I Believe in Me

Me A-Z
Positive Affirmations Book

RICH GROGAN

I Believe In Me: Alphabet Affirmations
Published by AME High Publishing LLC
Palmetto, FL

Copyright ©2022 by Rich Grogan. All rights reserved.

No part of this book may be reproduced in any form or by any mechanical means, including information storage and retrieval systems without permission in writing from the publisher/author, except by a reviewer who may quote passages in a review.

All images, logos, quotes, and trademarks included in this book are subject to use according to trademark and copyright laws of the United States of America.

ISBN: 978-0-9988490-4-1

Publisher's Cataloging-in-Publication data

Names: Grogan, Rich, author.
Title: I believe in me : alphabet affirmations / Rich Grogan, Master Martial Arts Instructor.
Description: Palmetto, FL: AME High Publishing LLC, 2022. | Summary: Plant the seeds of self-confidence and strengthen your child's self-belief and self-esteem with alphabet affirmations.
Identifiers: ISBN: 978-0-9988490-4-1
Subjects: LCSH Affirmations--Juvenile literature. | Self-talk in children. | Self-esteem--Juvenile literature. | Self-reliance--Juvenile literature. | Self-actualization (Psychology)--Juvenile literature. | Alphabet. | BISAC JUVENILE NONFICTION / Social Topics / Self-Esteem & Self-Reliance | JUVENILE NONFICTION / Social Issues / Emotions & Feelings
Classification: LCC BF697.5.S43 .G76 2022 | DDC 155.2--dc23

JUVENILE NONFICTION / Social Topics / Self-Esteem & Self-Reliance
Cover and Interior design by Victoria Wolf, copyright owned by Rich Grogan.

QUANTITY PURCHASES: Schools, companies, professional groups, clubs, and other organizations may qualify for special terms when ordering quantities of this title. For information, email bullyproof@grogansma.com.

All rights reserved by Rich Grogan. and AME High Publishing LLC.
Printed in the United States of America.

**For every child
a positive self image is the key to being strong**

*Thanks,
to God for the many blessings I've been given.*

*To my family,
Desi, Austin, Madelyn, Emmitt,
your love, patience and support have been my guiding light.*

*To my many mentors,
you have helped me believe in myself.*

A
I have an AMAZINGLY AWESOME ATTITUDE.

B
I am BRAVE.
I am BULLY proof.

I am COURAGEOUS and CONFIDENT.

D

I am DETERMINED to do my best.

I am EAGER to learn new things.

F I am FRIENDLY.
I am FUN to be around.

J

I bring JOY everywhere I go.

I am KIND.

L

I am LOVED.
I LOVE others.

I have MAGNIFICENT MANNERS.

N
I am NICE.
I am NEIGHBORLY.

I am a ONE and ONLY ORIGINAL.

P I am PROUD of who I am.

I am QUICK to help.

R

**I RESPECT myself.
I RESPECT others.**

T

I am TRUSTWORTHY.
I always TELL the TRUTH.

I am UNIQUE in UNIMAGINABLE ways.

V

I know how VALUABLE I am.

X

I make E**X**CEPTIONAL choices.

YOU can count on me.

Z

I am A-Z the best I can be.

ABOUT THE AUTHOR

MASTER RICH GROGAN, creator of the Grogan's Bully Proof System and best-selling author of *Becoming Bully Proof*, is on a mission to empower 10 million people with hope, faith & confidence to believe in themselves to stand up to every bully they face, both real & in their minds.

Master Grogan is passionate about bringing his unique, uplifting messages to audiences around the world because nothing is more vulnerable than someone who doesn't believe in themselves.

His experience with bullying as a child, parent, martial arts instructor and physical educator led him to understand that being able to defend oneself against bullying works from the inside-out, and is as easy as ABC.

Master Grogan is a 6th Degree Black Belt with over 40 years martial arts experience.

He has worked with kids for more than 35 years, coaching sports, teaching physical education in public schools and instructing martial arts. In addition he's the host of the Grogan's Bully Proof Podcast, a certified Ziglar Speaker & Life Coach, and the founder of Grogan's Martial Arts, one of the largest martial arts academies in the Midwest. He is a Christian, father of three and loving husband.

He would love the opportunity to empower your family, team or business with the hope and confidence to believe in themselves to stand out in the crowd and become bully proof.

To learn more about hiring Master Grogan as a speaker, or to buy his book and download a free copy of *The ABC's to Becoming Bully Proof* visit his website: **www.grogansbullyproof.com**

Follow on Social Media for free content & daily bully proof inspiration:

Facebook, Instagram, You-Tube, Tik Tok: @GrogansBullyProof

Email: bullyproof@grogansma.com

Twelve year old Logan is a quiet, big-hearted middle school kid who just wants to fit in. But, as it often happens, his kind heart is a magnet for bullies. Join us on an epic journey of highs and lows; with easy-to-follow lessons that will teach you, along with Logan, how to believe in yourself to become BULLY PROOF. Ages 9–15.

Available in paperback, Kindle, and Audible at AMAZON.COM

Made in the USA
Las Vegas, NV
05 November 2023

80306633R10021